The Second BEN WICKS Treasury

Also by Ben Wicks

Ben Wicks' Canada
Ben Wicks' Women
Ben Wicks' Book of Losers
Ben Wicks' Etiquette
More Losers
Wicks
Ben Wicks' Dogs
So You Want To Be Prime Minister
The First Ben Wicks Treasury
Mavis & Bill

The Second BEN WICKS Treasury

METHUEN

Toronto New York London Sydney Auckland

Canadian Cataloguing in Publication Data

Wicks, Ben, 1926–

    The second Ben Wicks treasury

ISBN 0-458-81150-5

1. Canadian wit and humor, Pictorial.   I. Title.

NC1449.W52A4   1987   741.5′971   C87-094195-X

Design/Don Fernley

Printed and Bound in Canada

1 2 3 4   87   91 90 89 88

To Doreen,
again with love.

Introduction

Since many thousands were unable to get *The First Ben Wicks Treasury* in their stocking two years ago, we have decided to issue *The Second Ben Wicks Treasury*. Does this mean that we have just slapped a different cover on a new version?

It does not.

The material contained in this book is all new (as they say on the box of soap suds).

But is it as good? Better. (The book, not the soap suds.) I now have my son, Vincent, working with me. Vincent has not only had the best teacher possible (what do you mean, "who"?), but he has brought to the cartoons a splash of youth. Which cartoons are Vincent's? I'm not saying, but here's a little tip. If there are any that you feel are not funny . . . need I say more?

Since *The First Ben Wicks Treasury* many people have asked why a book of this calibre is available only at Christmas. For the simple reason that this is what is known in the trade as a "stocking stuffer." Most stocking stuffers are designed for the boring shoe sizes 4 to 9; therefore, a whole bundle of avid readers had, before *The First Ben Wicks Treasury*, been completely overlooked. This book is designed for them —for those who wear sizes 14 to 18 or who have thin legs but enjoy wearing fat stockings.

Just one more reminder. For those of you who may be standing in a shop at this very moment ready to head for the counter with this stocking stuffer, I would remind you that most people have two legs. And as such, two stockings. Remember, two *Second Ben Wicks Treasuries* can be had for just double the price of one. Now take it to the cash register fast before someone else snatches it.

BEN WICKS

P.S. If you find that it does not fit the stocking you intended, try taking out a few pages.

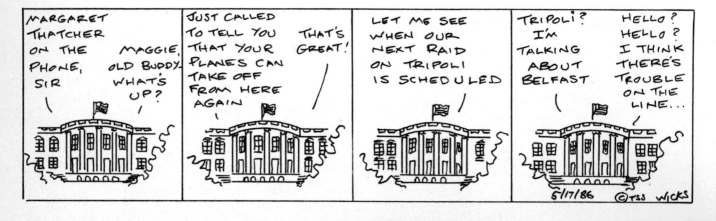

10

"It's a good thing for you I came home
early. You're missing Di and Charles."

"Of course you've seen this before. It's the news."

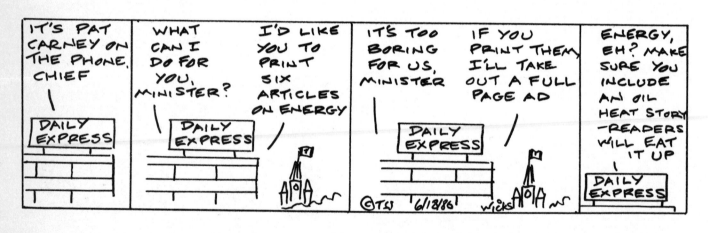

"Thank you, madam. Will that be all?"

"So much for the arrow test ban treaty."

"My father hated me so much, he left me the family farm."

"I told you smoking was bad for you."

"How come you never lose Mulroney's?"

"Keep complaining and your name won't go into the hat for the no-frills meal."

"You'll have to change your tune. You're still not using enough black notes, Mr. Botha."

"If the Americans hear about this, there'll be hell to pay."

"Can Billy come out to play?"

"Do you have anything by Bo Derek?"

"It can do the work of two men or one woman."

"It had to happen. I knew he'd forget it one morning if it wasn't screwed on."

"XTU to Pluto from Earth. No sign of intelligent life . . . over!"

"Okay, Mr. Dumpty. So you've tried the Berlin Wall — how about the Great Wall of China?"

"So much for modernizing the farm."

"Turner? We've got Sheila Copps. Do as we say or we'll release her."

"The one lobbying against lobbying may go in now."

23

"Oh yeah? Well I bet there would have been lots of people happy to hold hands with me."

"Why are *you* complaining? I came here to see someone off."

"What if Khadafy is out for the evening?"

"If we do decide to send a 'first wino' into
space, we'll contact you."

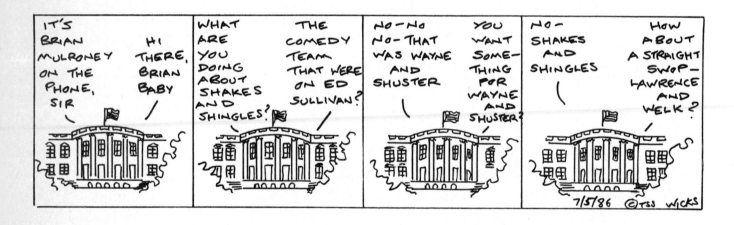

"They now have proof that Waldheim is
Hitler without a moustache."

"The following news bulletin has just been
handed to me . . . oh my God!"

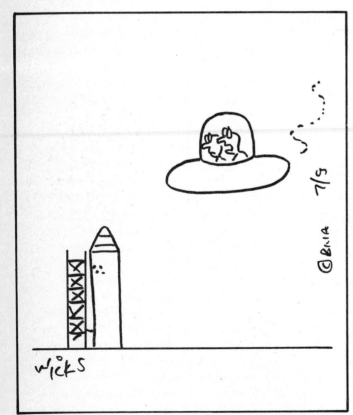

"Orders or no orders, I still say we land
and tell them where they went wrong."

"Of course it isn't necessary, but an
appendix transplant would be a first."

"There's only one way to reduce missiles.
Drop 'em on someone."

"It's for a cup of coffee to go with the
free food I'm getting at the food bank."

"Don't do it, Andy!"

"If Andy changes his mind tomorrow, tell
him he can get me at this number."

"So it's a cherry. Have you any idea of the price of apples?"

"Trust me. Merge and we'll be the biggest panhandlers on the block."

"How about a nice, little, one-owner two-seater?"

"All I said was, 'So far, so good.'"

"He says he can fix you but he must extra-bill."

"Before I let down my hair, how do I know you're not a terrorist?"

"We can't seem to agree on anything. He says Khadafy should be shot, I say he should be hanged."

"Whoopee! I've got enough air mile points to go to Paris with a companion of my choice."

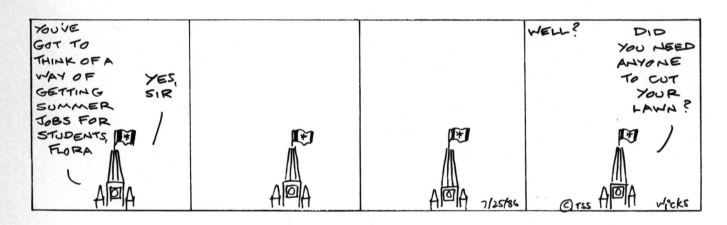

"Welcome to No-Frill Airlines. Now
hear this!"

"Damn, they've got the robots on their side."

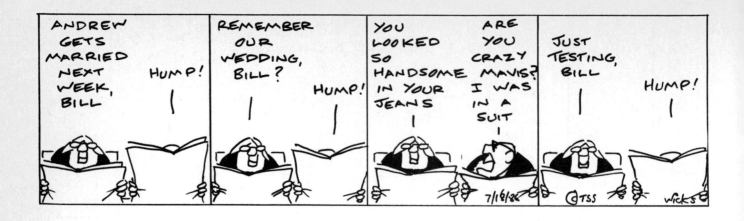

"The meaning went out of my life when
Meryl Streep made a comedy movie."

"To be honest, I have heard of a case where it
happened with a fly, but never this."

"The skinny girl Andrew married is on TV."

"Two for non-smoking."

"There seems to have been some mistake.
Are you really a lawyer or are you just
joking?"

"Is Di jealous of Fergie?"

"To start at the beginning, there's this
woman called Margaret Thatcher . . ."

"Are you sure this is for John Crosbie's mother?"

"More? What did you do with the last $100 million I sent you?"

"I never said I liked what Khadafy was doing. I just said we should support him."

"Margaret Thatcher is coming! Margaret Thatcher is coming!"

45

"You're making a big mistake. I'm not even a tourist."

"Okay, so we quit taking drugs.
What then?"

"Have you any idea how miserable your life will be if they bring in sanctions against South Africa?"

"You'll love the house. It's made of marijuana with cocaine windows and a heroin chimney."

"At the sound of the tone leave your obscene call, and breathe slowly, please."

"Sure you should continue to help the Contras, Ron. But are you sure you've got the right Mrs. Thatcher?"

"Okay, I like it. Now what's your nuclear bomb–carrying capability?"

"Good news. We've got a nibble from the New Democratic Party."

"The good news is that General Dynamics claim they can make them for $150,000 each."

"You've kicked the habit . . . no, hold it! Yes . . . no . . . you've started smoking again."

"Okay, it's agreed. We'll destroy one of our little flags if you destroy one of your little flags."

"It's a pre-summit, George. You won't need to tread softly and carry a big stick."

"He's about 5′ 10″. Dark hair, brown eyes. Comes in here all the time."

"If those evil, snide, brutal commies want cheap wheat, they've come to the right place."

"Remind me — did we have children who grew
up and left home?"

THE POLLS LIE — 3 OUT OF 5 DO NOT WANT ME OUT

THE CABINET IS WITH YOU, P.M

AND IF PEOPLE DO SAY THAT THEY'RE LYING —

— AND IF THERE IS ONE THING I CAN'T STAND IT'S LYING — YOU ALL LIKE THE WAY I'M DOING THINGS, DON'T YOU?

9/8/86

ER — NICE VOICE

LIKE THE SUIT

WHERE'S DALTON

WHO WANTS COFFEE?

©TSS   Wicks

ISN'T IT WONDERFUL — IF THERE WAS A VOTE HELD TODAY I'D BE THE TOP DOG —

— THE BIG CHEESE — THE HEAD HONCHO —

— NO ONE COULD TELL ME WHAT TO DO

HAVE YOU TAKEN OUT THAT GARBAGE YET?

JUST DOING IT, DEAR

9/9/86   ©TSJ   Wicks

"Compared with other throne speeches I felt that the delivery lacked animation."

"Well, another day, another 72.40¢ U.S."

"See! I told you we should have left home without them."

"You may find our incentive methods unusual, but they do work."

"It's the peasants, sire. They've found a way of making gold out of dirt and filth."

"It's agreed then. We support the President and reluctantly agree to continue to trade with Libya."

"Careful, dear. You may get Joan Rivers."

DR WO
PLASTIC
SURGEON

"I can't help it if farmers throw things at you. It was your idea to look like the prime minister, Mr. Brown."

"Dear Ron. We need 100 million bucks to overthrow our leader . . . no, make that 'commie' leader."

"Do you, Margaret Thatcher, take Pieter
Botha . . ."

"Before we try a transplant we'd better decide. Are we looking for a size 8 or size 13?"

"Ron, baby! It's your old pal, Mikhail . . . how about some more cheap wheat, old buddy?"

"Don't tell me. I know the face. Beirut, August 1986, right?"

"If you don't want to get high, what do you want to do?"

I'M SICK OF POLLS THAT SAY BRIAN IS UNPOPULAR—

DID THEY ASK MY OPINION?— NO! DID THEY ASK YOUR OPINION?— NO! AND DO YOU KNOW WHY?

BECAUSE THEY'RE NOT INTERESTED IN INTELLIGENT, INFORMED OPINION—THAT'S WHY

BUT IF THEY ASKED ME I WOULD HAVE SAID... I'M NOT INTERESTED, MAVIS

DESPITE THE PRICE HIKES WE STILL HAVE A PROBLEM WITH THE OIL INDUSTRY   WHY DON'T YOU PHONE OTTAWA, DON?

GEE— DO YOU THINK I SHOULD?   SURE I DO—

—DON'T FORGET— YOU'RE THE PREMIER OF ALBERTA   YOU'RE RIGHT— I'LL CALL

BRIAN? THIS IS DON GETTY   I AM OUT OF THE OFFICE— AT THE SOUND OF THE TONE— PLEASE LEAVE YOUR MESSAGE ... THANK YOU, DON

"Couldn't we get rid of apartheid and call it
something else?"

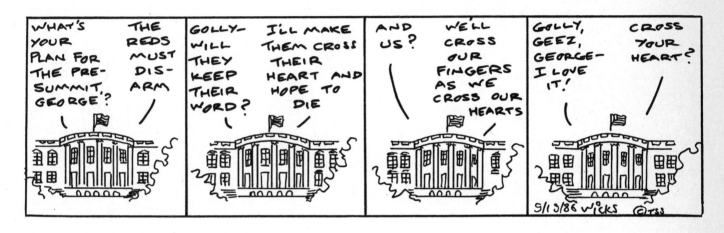

"I call it arms limitation. We're each
limited to one hit and I go first."

"Why is it that what's in your section is always more interesting than what's in mine?"

"Remind me — am I going to work or just getting home?"

"Whatever happened to the guys who sold pencils?"

"And this was for volunteering to serve in Paris."

"Good grief, Mavis! How many more times must I tell you not to phone me at the office?"

"He pushes stuff to other humans that they buy to make themselves sick. How about your master?"

"Hands up!"

"Notice how the artist kept between the lines and covered the little numbers with paint?"

"You're missing film of the opening of Parliament."

"Ask him how much it would cost to build one between our house and Thatcher's."

"Oh, Ahmad, isn't it exciting? Our first visit to Paris!"

"They need a pusher on the corner of Seventh and Main."

"Okay, okay. If I stop smoking will you
marry me?"

WITH THE P.M OUT OF THE COUNTRY NOW'S THE TIME TO GET TOUGH | RIGHT ON, JOHN

WHO'S IN CHARGE? | NIELSEN

5/13/86

WHEN DOES MULRONEY GET BACK?

©TSS

wicks

THIS IS A BIG DAY FOR THE PRIME MINISTER, BILL — BOTH ALBERTA AND QUEBEC GO TO THE POLLS

I'M NOT WORRIED— ONCE THE PEOPLE LOOK AT BRIAN'S RECORD THEY'LL SEE WHAT HAS HAPPENED SINCE HE TOOK OVER —

— THEY'LL MAKE THE RIGHT DECISION BY LOOKING AT THE FACTS

9/29/86 ©TSS

GEE, THAT'S A SHAME— I THINK THEY SHOULD GIVE HIM ANOTHER CHANCE | IT'S LUCKY FOR YOU, MAVIS, THAT YOU'VE ALREADY WON ME OVER

wicks

"You have been found guilty of spying.
Have you anything to say before you
arrive in Russia?"

"I'll have to call you back. I think the
terrorists are at it again."

"Don't forget to wave, dear."

". . . and don't forget to pick up a packet of
white stuff on your way home."

"It's from a Keith Davey, thanking you for your advice on how to sell his book."

". . . and as for Chrétien's threat, I think Turner is justified in overreacting."

"It's Gorbachev. In keeping with our new warning agreement, he's letting us know that 5,000 missiles will be here in 3½ minutes."

"I think you took a wrong turn somewhere. This is for someone called Contra."

71

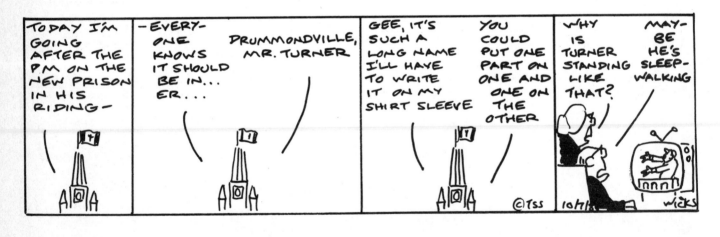

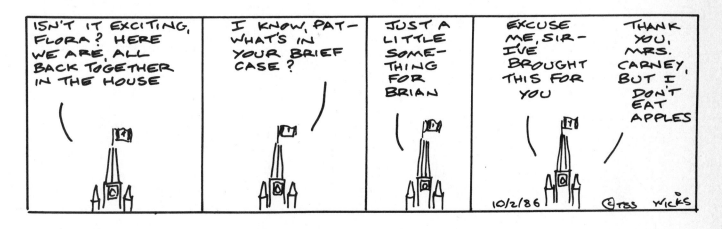

"In the event of a star war, place the
cyanide mask over the mouth . . ."

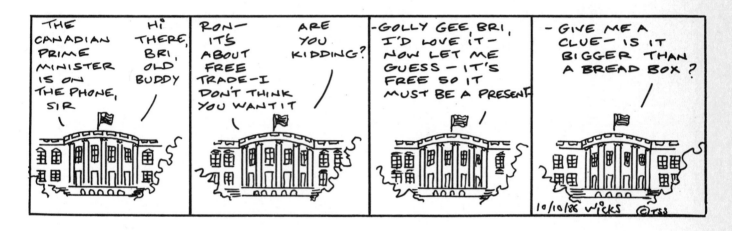

"Have you considered the CIA?"

"I want you to be honest, Frank. As your
wife, do I understand you?"

"Before we talk business, are you sure
you're not South African?"

"What will it be? Politics, sports or a
snappy one-liner to get the juices going?"

"Have you considered writing a book?"

"I know they're harmful but I still can't kick the habit."

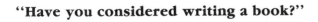

"Smoking or non-smoking?"

"No, no Ron! When I mentioned free trade I didn't mean Nancy for Mila."

"Sure I've tried grass. But have you tried dandelions?"

"I'll agree to a leg control treaty if you will."

"You see. I told you there would be no form of
intelligent life."

"It's your own fault. You shouldn't have
called her 'baby!' "

"Oh, well. Back to the drawing board."

"Do you realize how serious this is, Harold? If the U.N. goes broke we'll have to work for a living."

"I know what you're thinking but I can't stop."

"Those of you who feel they could do a better job, make yourselves known."

"Friends . . ."

"Those of you planning a career in politics will find this disease quite interesting."

"Just for a laugh, try some disinformation."

"We'll wait for them to sign their disarmament agreement then let it rip."

"Yippee! No more dieting!"

**"There's been a mix-up. We've just tossed
six of our spies out of the Kremlin."**

"Put me down as undecided."

"How do I know you're not giving me
disinformation just to scare me?"

"Hi! It's me again . . ."

"It was terrible. I dreamt I was Tom
Cruise . . . at 98!"

"But we gave you food two years ago."

"Good evening. There was no news today and this is Knowlton Nash reading it."

"Did the Jones' cat send our cat one last year?"

"Better do what their tourists are doing. Avoid the Middle East."

"Isn't that nice? Reagan has included a 'Peace on earth, goodwill to all men' card."

89

"I can't speak now, I'm watching the
Refrigerator."

"And now for the best acting in a show seen
by the least number of Canadians . . ."

"I quit!"

"Acid rain is coming . . ."

"When I said, 'Up the Hill,' I was asking for a book, not expressing a personal opinion."

"Dear President Reagan. We, the Contras, are still waiting for the $100 million . . . $100,000 . . . $50,000 . . . 50 bucks . . ."

"After doing a cost analysis with a three-year projection, I've decided to live at home again."

"And now for the results of the king look-alike contest."

"If I do kiss you, what proof do I have that you'll change into Mayor Eastwood?"

"You're missing Mulroney in Korea."

"I think it's time we faced facts. These arms talks are a sham."

"I'm sorry. I wasn't listening. What did you say last year?"

"It's Reagan. He's going to blast you over
Afghanistan again. Is that okay?"

"And this one tried to hit me up for fifty bucks."

"The group that we wiped out are firing back . . . over."

"You're too late. We've settled."

"Fill her up!"

"Tell us again about the time you made North Americans line up for gas, Abdul."

". . . to my cousin Maude, who always told me how much she liked animals . . ."

"They were going to put me in solitary but there were too many in there already."

"It's Winnie Mandella. Since you won't let her live in her own house she's moved into yours."

MULRONEY SHOULD STOP FEELING HE HAS TO ANSWER THE MEDIA FOR EVERY ACTION—

—HE SHOULD GET ONE OF HIS FLUNKIES TO ANSWER FOR HIM

SUNSHINE HOME

11/13/86

WHY ARE YOU LEAVING YOUR GREENS, MRS TRAVIS?

IF YOU'RE WAITING FOR ME TO ANSWER, MAVIS, FORGET IT!

7

©TSS WICKS

THE FORGET COMMISSION RECOMMENDS SAVING MONEY BY REDUCING THE STAFF AT UNEMPLOYMENT HEAD OFFICE

WON'T THAT RESULT IN MORE UN-EMPLOYMENT, BILL?

MAYBE—BUT THEY'LL SAVE MONEY

BUT MORE PEOPLE WILL BE GETTING UNEMPLOYMENT CHECKS

NOT IF THERE'S NOONE AROUND TO GIVE THEM OUT

©TSS

BOY—THAT FORGET SHOULD BE P.M.

OR MINISTER OF FINANCE

11/12/86 WICKS

2/17

"Charge! Let's take this hill for the Ayatollah."

"I hear he was a door-to-door salesman."

"Some guy named Ed McMahon wants to give you $10 million, whatever they are."

"Don't tell me. I know the face. You're . . ."

"Okay, we'll agree to another spy swap, but how do I know you're not a real tree?"

"Heil, Uranus."

"Someone told him he could see Halley's Comet with the naked eye."

"On October 30, 1965, you lied about your travel expenses. True or false?"

"Strange. I was told that earth people had two legs."

"If the blacks don't like life in South Africa,
they should go back to where they
came from."

"But if you're involved in arms around the world, you must meet Gloria. She was with Hands Across America."

"Congratulations. You have been carefully chosen for the next suicide mission."

"And what if this McDermott guy is no longer sympathetic to workers' demands?"

"Good news, dear. They're going to replace your Audi 5000 with a new one."

"I'm sorry, Mr. Botha. I still see tall, *dark* handsome men. No white."

"And if Khadafy turns around before you can pin it on him, run like hell."

"Looks great. But what makes you think Khadafy will agree to come?"

"Gee, no kidding. My dad works at looking for a job, too."

"Did you tell them that cut-backs or not, you
needed a bed?"

I THINK FORGET'S REPORT ON UNEMPLOYMENT IS RIGHT—

—PEOPLE SHOULD BE PAID FOR WORKING NOT LAYING AROUND, MAVIS

THEY'RE NOT LAYING AROUND, BILL— THEY'RE IN A TRANSITIONAL PHASE BETWEEN SHORT TERM FLUID MARGINAL REDUNDANCY

SO HOW COME THEY HAVE TIME FOR FISHING?

11/22/86 ©TSS WICKS

NOW DON'T FORGET, MAVIS, WE LEAVE EARLY— SO START SAYING GOODNIGHT AT 9 OCLOCK—

—IF YOU DON'T I SHALL START DISCUSSING FREE TRADE

WHATEVER HAPPENED TO REYKJAVIK- SAKHAROV AND SOVIET DISSIDENT RATUSHINSKAYA?

I'VE FORGOTTEN MY TEETH

MAKES SENSE

11/20/86 ©TSS WICKS

2/23

"Khashoggi? I need more arms. And while you're at it, throw in a few legs."

"What do you mean, 'Have you heard about
the big seat sale?'"

"I still say we should put it in our Swiss account along with the rest, Ferdinand."

"Excuse me, sir. You've just crossed off yourself."

"An unexpectedly hasty departure by the company treasurer has resulted in a disappointing annual financial report."

"And tell them that if they don't reduce their arms, next time you'll be carrying an explosive device."

"You call *that* a gun?"

"Mr. Marcos will see you now."

"If you quit smoking, drinking and lay off women, you may live to 25."

"How do I know it's not from South Africa?"

"What makes you think that you can bring
back Canadian football fans?"

"It was terrible. I dreamed I'd kidnapped Marcos and nobody wanted him back."

"Smoking, non-smoking or trying to quit?"

"It was working fine until Ferdinand Marcos appeared on the screen."

"Then the lovely Imelda gathered all her shoes together, returned to the Philippines and lived happily ever after."

"Have you any skills other than the ability
to give away toys?"

"I fell off a roof."

"What do you mean you're out of myrrh?
You can't be out of myrrh!"

"For Pete's sake, stop crying. He'll do what
he always does, catch us on the way back."

"You were observed climbing down a
number of chimneys on December 25th.
How do you plead?"

"You just missed them."

"It's been our experience that a war theme
is not a good sell at this time of year."

"I'd like a raise."

"This short fat man on the roof that you see . . . does he have anything for me?"

"What did you get for Christmas?"

"Yes, Virginia, there is a Santa Claus."